There are 25 species of chipmunks in the world.

All species are found in North America except for one that lives in Asia.

# CHIPMUNKS!

## A MY INCREDIBLE WORLD PICTURE BOOK

MY INCREDIBLE WORLD

Copyright © 2018, My Incredible World

All rights reserved. This book or any portion thereof may not be reproduced or used in any manner whatsoever without the express written permission of the copyright holder.

www.myincredibleworld.com

**Photos Licensed Under CC BY 2.0. Full terms at https://creativecommons.org/licenses/by/2.0:**
Page 5. "Chipmunk" by Marilyn Peddle, available at https://www.flickr.com/photos/marilynjane/4729836479
Page 7. "Cliff Chipmunk" by Andy Reago & Chrissy McClarren, available at https://www.flickr.com/photos/wildreturn/33981189526
Page 8. "Petit suisse -- Little chipmunk" by Gilles Gonthier, available at https://www.flickr.com/photos/gillesgonthier/8770139581
Page 12. "Petit suisse -- Little chipmunk" by Gilles Gonthier, available at https://www.flickr.com/photos/gillesgonthier/8917688627
Page 13. "Tamia rayé -- Eastern chipmunk" by Gilles Gonthier, available at https://www.flickr.com/photos/gillesgonthier/8250472195
Page 14. "Gray Collared Chipmunk?" by Greg Schechter, available at https://www.flickr.com/photos/gregthebusker/8038078451
Page 15. "20170323_2328" by dw_ross, available at https://www.flickr.com/photos/dw_ross/33484892891
Page 16. "Tamia rayé -- Eastern chipmunk" by Gilles Gonthier, available at https://www.flickr.com/photos/gillesgonthier/7368747352
Page 18. "Chipmunk in Zion" by Tydence Davis, available at https://www.flickr.com/photos/tydence/28413423256
Page 19. "chipmunk" by Paul Dunleavy, available at https://www.flickr.com/photos/dunleavy_family/3497981074
Page 20. "chipmunk" by Michal Adamczyk, available at https://www.flickr.com/photos/koczkodan/23811051178
Page 21. "Petit suisse -- Little chipmunk" by Gilles Gonthier, available at https://www.flickr.com/photos/gillesgonthier/8189652676
Page 22. "Yellowstone Chipmunk" by Bernd Thaller, available at https://www.flickr.com/photos/bernd_thaller/39479600654

**Photos Licensed Under CC BY-SA 2.0. Full terms at https://creativecommons.org/licenses/by-sa/2.0:**
Page 2. "Chipmunk" by Jerry Friedman, available at https://www.flickr.com/photos/10904042@N04/27316995295
Page 11. "Chipmunk" by Johnathan Nightingale, available at https://www.flickr.com/photos/johnath/4783913906

**Other Photo Credits:**
Page 1. Untitled by Sylvia Barron, available at https://unsplash.com/photos/mnr9sWuZHBQ
Page 3. Untitled by Forest Simon, available at https://unsplash.com/photos/yolrxKeWztzk
Page 4. Untitled by Evan McDougall, available at https://unsplash.com/photos/25Kj6bGtEO0
Page 6. Untitled by Tony Fortunato, available at https://unsplash.com/photos/chs4FinGDQQ
Page 9. "IMG_2828" by Tyler Brenot, available at https://www.flickr.com/photos/152474924@N02/24018699948
Page 10. Untitled by Twinkal Solanki, available at https://unsplash.com/photos/T4olOJqVmWk
Page 17. "Tamia 021" by André Chivinski, available at https://www.flickr.com/photos/chivinskia/37296681184

The Greek word for chipmunk is tamias, which means "treasurer."

Most chipmunks have stripes on their head, back and tail.

Chipmunks are onmivores, meaning they eat both plants and meat.

Chipmunks live in large underground burrow systems up to 30 feet long!

Their burrows have separate rooms to store nuts and seeds for winter!

Chipmunks have cheek pouches that stretch up to 3 times their head size!

Chipmunks usually weigh between 1 and 5 ounces.

Chipmunks can reach about 8 to 10 inches long, including their tails.

Baby chipmunks are called pups.

Mother chipmunks can have litters of 2 to 8 pups twice a year!

In the wild, most chipmunks live to be about 2 to 3 years old.

A group of chipmunks is called a scurry.

Chipmunks are excellent climbers!

Surprisingly, chipmunks are good swimmers, too!

Chipmunks do not hibernate, but they sleep for longer periods during winter.

Chipmunks' natural enemies include hawks, snakes, weasels and foxes.

Chipmunks are solitary animals, meaning they prefer to live alone.

Chipmunks are very territorial & guard their burrows from other chipmunks.

Chipmunks can communicate using chirping noises!

Chipmunks are incredible!

Made in the USA
Monee, IL
29 March 2023